I Don't Want Want
To Be Rich,
Just Able

I Don't Want To Be Rich, Just Able

Poems by

CAROL PREJEAN ZIPPERT

NEWSOUTH BOOKS

Montgomery

NewSouth Books
P.O. Box 1588
Montgomery, AL 36102

Library of Congress Cataloging-in-Publication Data
Zippert, Carol Prejean
I don't want to be rich, just able / Carol Zippert
p. cm.
ISBN 1-58838-058-0
1. Afro-American women—poetry. 2. Afro-Americans—Poetry.
I. Title
PS3576.I567I2 1997
811'.54—dc21 97-1442

SECOND PRINTING

Printed in the United States of America
by Phoenix Color Corporation

For you, Mother (Edolia Richard Prejean)
and for you, Daddy (Oran Prejean), as you rest.
Thank you for your love.

This collection is a special treasure for me.
I proudly dedicate it to the two persons
who first made my being a treasure.

The title of my book is taken from my mother's
everyday philosophies. As a child I was attentive to the
insights and perceptions through which she defined her
world. Then I scarcely understood my mother's wisdom,
but I held on to it.

I don't want to be rich, just able.
Able to care for my family
Able to work for my church.
Able to prepare my roots and herbs
to care for the sick in the community.
Able to bake my homemade breads and cakes
and serve lots of food when visitors come.
Able to tend my garden, my chickens, ducks,
and rabbits.
Able to meet my debts and keep my good name.

Contents

Loving

He Was There

He was there
He was just there
He didn't come
looking for me
And I didn't know
that I needed him
But he was there
and made all the difference

Let Me Give

Let me make your world star-lit
and cleanse it with moist dew
and herbal freshness

Let me thin out the fog
and sprinkle rainbow hues
at random

Let me transform your storms
and welcome the light, cool
invigorating rain

Let me revive those life-carrying
veins
that allow your heart to keep rhythm
with life's pulsating forces

Let me temper your despair
and resignation

Let me give you new birth
and hope

Let me give you dreams
with bright smiles and laughter
that will make your today
reach tomorrow

Let me give you love
binding love that's free
to endure through all your moments

Let me give you me
Let me give you
Let me give

Wearing the Crown

Were it given to me
to direct the sun and
position the stars in the skies
as I so pattern
I would not feel so empowered
As I am
through the strength
of your love

Were it given to me
to control the seas and
the tides that beckon to the moon
I would not feel so honored
As I am
through the return
of your love

Were it given to me
to bud the trees in springtime and
call forth every species of flower
in the colors of my dreams
I would not find such delight
As I do
through the peace
of your love

Were it given to me
to transform storms and
paint rainbows at random
with just a simple smile
I would not be so enriched
As I am
through the perception
of your love

Were it given to me
to wear the crown of justice
and
calm the fears of humankind
As the bearer of freedom
I could not sense the same
majesty
As I do
through the depths
of your love

Were it given to me
to choose a love
to last forever and more
I choose you

When You Give Me You

When you've given me
a little
You've given me
you
When you've given me
everything
You've given me
you

When you've searched for
a gift
You've given me
that wish
When you've longed for
those words
You've given me
those thoughts

When you've wanted to
show me
I've felt your need
When you've wanted to
love me
I've shared that bliss

When you've given me
you
You've given me
everything

A Sacred Medium

Sometimes I want to
write a poem
to say I love you
A poem that says
you're wonderful—special
a treasure beyond my dreams
So I give you
every poem I write
to say I love you.

Just Loving Silly

This woman should be silly
for loving a man so dearly
She should know her heart was meant
to care but not to consent
to give her mind, breath and soul
in trust for him to cherish, to hold

This woman should be silly
for needing his love so clearly
She should remember to stay aloft
finding safety in appearing tough
never allowing that he may know
it is his love that provides the glow

This woman should be silly
for sharing a gift so freely
She should have known they'd be a
power
loving with him, they are a tower
They build onto each other's strengths
and grow as lovers and as friends

This woman can't be silly
for loving a man so dearly
She does know her heart was meant
to care and to consent
For she loves with all she is
hoping to match the love he gives

I Met A Man

I met a man today
for the first time, I think
And he was clear, and different,
and new
For none of the reasons I know

I met a man today
for the first time, I think
And he was gentle, and warm,
and safe
For all the reasons I want

I met a man today
for the first time, I think
And he commanded feelings, and motion,
and trust
For all the reasons I need

I met a man today
for the first time, I think
And he gave me his hand, and his heart,
and his mind
For all the reasons that are right

I met a man today
for the first time, I think
And we began to live
For the first time, I think

Unconditional Love

You can never have
too much of me
You can never have
so much
that I will say
there is no more

Boundlessness

It is easy to love
in your dreams
You are your own
matchmaker
But it is so powerful
to dream in your love
You are the choicemaker

Unruly Love

I told this unruly love
to keep its wanderings
in my soul
I told this love
to bear its housing
in my heart
I told this love
to hold its song
in my eyes
I told this love
to harbor our secrets
and hoard our joy
I told this unruly love
to wait
to smile in silence
But I share a love
that will not
be contained
So what shall I tell
such an unruly love

Has Anybody Ever

Has anybody ever
just been crazy about you
Has anybody ever
lived like you are
the center of their universe
Has anybody ever
looked forward to greeting
a day because you were
in that sunshine
And has anybody ever
hastened to savor a sunset
because your presence
lined that horizon
Has anybody ever
committed the rest of their life
to caring for you and helping you
realize your dreams
And has anybody ever
found their greatest joy
in just knowing you are happy
Has anybody
Ever
received such powerful special love
from you
Has anybody ever

He Singled Me

I try to think, what
did he teach me
Were there lessons I
wrote down or ones I
pressed into my brain
vowing never to forget
I try to think, how
did he inspire me
Were there experiences
that transferred into a
forming value or just a
slight of silence that
conveyed a truth
I try to think, what
did he give me
Was there more than the
shelter and nourishment as
benefits of his daily labors
or were there gifts that
singled me and confirmed
that he did care
I try to think, what
did he leave me
Is it his usual quiet
weighed down with his
struggles

Is it his peculiar humor
lifting those same lives
Is it the comfort of feeling
that even when he wasn't there
I could know he would come
back
I try to think, what
made him so special that
I wish I had given him more

No Barricade To Love

When you love me
in your pain
is there still a smile
in your heart

When you love me
in your pain
is there still hope
in your soul

When you love me
in your pain
Can you still hear music
in the wind
Can you still find poetry
in the flowers,
Can your sun
still raise its warmth

When you love me
in your pain
Can you still love me
in your pain

Lifting Children

My Boy

My boy here
is gon be
a man one day
He gon be
a man
soon one day

I ain't gon
be saying
Boy, tie them shoes
Cause this man
gon be walking
in them shoes
getting where
he needs to be

And I ain't gon
be saying
Boy, wash them hands
Cause it don't matter
if his hands is clean
when this man is
reaching out to
comfort where
he needs to be

I won't need
to be saying

Boy, raise them shoulders
Cause this man's head
is gon be
keeping them straight
directing his
whole self where
he needs to be

My boy here
is gon be
a man one day
He gon be
a man
soon one day

Then he be saying
Mama, there's some
changin need be done
There's some freedom
need be gotten
and some living
we been missing
And that gon be
a man talking

My boy here is
gon be
a man one day
He gon be
a man
soon one day

Hope Chest

Go from me and
take from me
one lifetime of all collected
treasures of a hope chest

I gave you birth
but I owe you life

Awesomeness

I felt her deep in thoughts
I approached in awe
I said:
What are your plans for tomorrow
She said:
I can't see myself in the future
I said:
Don't you have dreams—what are
your dreams
She said:
They don't go beyond today or this
moment
I stood in shock
I thought:
What happens to the young
who have no dreams to protect
What happens to the young
who have no dreams to lose
What happens to us
who have no youth
who dream
What happens

Sleep, Child

Sleep child, sleep
Tomorrow needs you
and that day won't have
no more time in it
than this one
And you'll have to move through it
like it's the last day you've got
Sleep child, sleep
You'll have to meet that morning
with the sun rising through you
Shining from your eyes
Glowing in your hair
Warming by your touch
You'll have to tread over this earth
scratching at a dry, barren land
A once rich soil loosened by misuse and no use
You'll have to wade in waters
stagnant and disease-breeding
and shiver in a rain that stings
when it should refresh
Sleep child, sleep
But know that this coming day
won't greet you alone
There'll be footprints
Some are there to lead you
Others are there to guide you not to follow

But the important footprints
are yours
As you step you form that day
like clay
that's been smoothed into a ball
not telling what it once was
but ready for new shapes and forms
Ready for you to mold this day
Sleep, child sleep
Tomorrow needs you
and that day won't have
no more time in it
than this one

The School Bus

The school bus doesn't
stop at my house
anymore
But my morning still carries
the rumbling, creaking sounds
alerting me of its approach
My ears follow as the bus
pounces on my street
breaking in fizzing halts
signaling each pick-up point
I hear the jerking doors
open and close swallowing
the laughing dancing voices
I listen for the quiet when
the bus descends the hill only
to turn and rumble through my street
again by the same route
not satisfied that it reminded me
once already
that the school bus
doesn't stop
at my house anymore
But there are still
children
who need to ride

From A Child's Soul

Sometimes I wonder
if I could be a child again
feeling like the world was made for me
to find out why it was made at all
Sometimes I wonder
if I could be a child again
asking those questions in an innocence
that says I really want to know:
What is blue?
What makes water wet?
How do we know when it's not still yesterday?
Why can't you see things when you sleep
with your eyes open?
Do flowers talk to each other?
Sometimes I wonder
if I could be a child again
not waiting for someone else's answers
but creating my own
Sometimes I wonder
can only children do that

God's Child

The child was born amidst
flowers, smiles and sunshine
He was God's child
He brought gifts of laughter,
hopes and joy
He was God's child

The child struggled through
storms, unrest and sadness
He was God's child
We gave him our love,
our patience and our understanding
He was God's child

The child grew to a man
still searching for treasures,
puzzling over life's mysteries
and reaching for promises of happiness—
promises made only to God's child
And he was God's child

The child grew tired and prayed for rest
We offered him our strength to guide him
We offered him our lives to support him
He was God's child
And he found his peace with God

Now when we hear birds sing
and smell spring flowers
When we feel the warm rays of sun
and the cool refreshing rain,
we will remember our child

And when we see bright smiles
and share our laughter
we will remember our child
And because of our own faith in God
we will always believe
He is God's child

When She Was Only 13

She's only 13
She resisted her parents
and fought her siblings
They reprimanded her
and belittled her
So she sneaked a beer
and consumed it in her closet

She avoided her teachers
and shunned her classmates
They judged her
and labeled her
So she sneaked another beer
and consumed it in her closet

She grew and gained weight
and felt she was no longer pretty
She disliked herself
She pitied herself
So she sneaked more beer
and consumed them in her closet

Her parents and teachers worried
Her siblings and classmates laughed
Her grades plummeted
Her esteem was gone
So she gradually sneaked into a wine bottle
and alcohol began to consume her

Her parents ask why
but are afraid to know why
Her teachers say she's just bad
and expect nothing of her

Her peers are now curious
How does she get away with it
Everyone has something to say
But only the beer and wine listen

She's only 13
and she doesn't know
how she got so old
She's only 13
and she doesn't know
who would want her to reach 14
So she retreats to her closet
and gives the only day of her life
to beer and wine

Maybe today someone will wake up
and hear her struggle
Maybe today someone will reach out
and extend a heart
hoping she will feel the love
She's only 13
Give her today

What Will I Tell Cydney

What will I tell
my grandchild
About the victim
Rodney King
About the verdict
L.A. Police
About the justice
U.S.A.
What will I tell
my grandchild
About the victim
homeless black man
About the verdict
Birmingham skinheads
About the justice
U.S.A.
What will I tell
Little Cydney
About the KKK
on Dr. King's road sign
About us and her
the victims

About rising racism
the verdict
About the U.S.A.
the justice
What will I tell
Cydney
About all the things
that I don't want her to know

As I See You

Sometimes I think of you
and I see me
I see those little things
you do
that act like me
I sense some thoughts
about you
that feel like me
I think of you
so I move in your rhythm
and it could be my music
I listen
as your eyes sing
and it could be my tune
I absorb
the melody of your scores
as I dance in your smile
I look at you
I look at all of you
and I know for sure
that a note, a tone may sound
of me
But you are your own
song
Sometimes
I think of you
and I see you

Gaining In Losing

I have only what you are
I hope for only what you can be
I let you go
to be you
And so to be a part of me
Always

Don't Play God With Me

Don't play God with me
just 'cause I'm a child
You say you have the right
to tell me what to do,
the right to tell me what to say
and where to go
But I see your own indecisions
I hear you tear yourself down
and I watch you hide from the things
you ought to change

Don't play God with me
just 'cause I'm a child
You say that you prayed for my birth
so you could teach me to build
a strong person in myself
But you've internalized your bondage
You've abandoned the spirituality
of your culture
You've not kept the vigil in honor of
those who died for you
and you've failed to build a legacy
that I could follow

Don't play God with me
just 'cause I'm a child

You were entrusted to secure your rights,
win your justice and build your peace
and that would be my foundation for living
But you send me to schools
that imprison my spirit
You lock me in classrooms
that deny my imagination
You give me a curricula of drugs,
weapons, violence and disrespect
and you say this is my education

Don't play God with me
just 'cause I'm a child
Don't promise me that you'll
make me a perfect new world
and that you'll give me the stars,
the moon and the mountains
God already gave me those
Don't promise me a life
without struggle
and don't promise me that I'll
live happily ever after on earth
Even God didn't promise me that

Just show me that you believe
in yourself
and that you have a commitment
beyond yourself
Just allow me the chance to learn
Allow me the resources to grow

Just live with me so that I can know
that every other child
of every other color
is my sister and my brother

Don't play God with me
Because I am God's child

Dreaming A World

Looking Up For Flowers

Why aren't there
flowers in the sky
Why not
Is not anything
possible?

Why aren't there flowers
in the clouds
Silly
Then it would rain
flowers
And folk would complain
Flowers in their hair
Flowers on their laundry
Flowers on the windshields
of their cars
Flowers everywhere

So why aren't there
flowers in the clouds?

Dancer

I want to be a dancer
And stretch my arms, my legs,
my long, long neck
to reach around this world
to touch all within this world
I want to be a dancer

When the Poem Writes Me

This is a day I don't want
to write a poem
This is a day I don't need
to say it in print
This is a day I just want
the sun on my face
and the wind in my eyes
and feel the poem
in my soul

Out Of This World

One day like today
I look into the world and
there is no color there
Where once was life,
forms and shapes float
like shadows of a past

One day like today
I reach into the world and
there is no scent there
Where once was flower,
stillness holds the air
like a burnt forest

One day like today
I move into the world and
there is no warmth there
Where once was smile,
sharp stones are underfoot
like a winter wind

One day like today
I step into the world and
it's not there

Turning The World Right Side Up

When I feel
your world
is upside down
My world
falls apart

When I see
your hurt
spread across your face
My pain
is unbearable

When I know
your disappointments
have shaken your goals
My hopes
Are drained

When I sense
your need
for understanding
My struggles
reach out to you

When it seems
nothing is approaching
your dreams
We can have comfort
in each other

When at last
the overcast lifts
We will grow
the stronger
for it

The Sunset

The Lord gave me
a sunset one day
He clasped his hands
around the blues, greens, browns
and yellows of His earth
and spreading them apart again
created a flaming, dripping,
flashing burst of
color across the sky
His palms moving gently
over the already electrifying canvas
left hints of violet and baby blue
designing that subtle calm
among the dazzling blends
of orange and gold
The Lord gave me
a sunset one day
of nothing but dust and reflection
The Lord gave
me
a sunset
one day
Did you
see it

Living My Stories

I like to tell myself stories
They be so powerful sometimes
I can make myself laugh and dance
or I can make myself cry and fret
I can make myself be all over this planet
or I can make myself invisible in a crowd
I like to tell myself stories
I can develop a host of characters
whose lives are designed not to change history
but to make today worth the histories we have
I like to tell myself stories
They can blossom as I choose
They can be as I know things are
or they can be as I make things out
I like to tell myself stories
They can be so powerful sometimes
I just got to know
the stories I live
and those I don't

Cats

Cats !
Felines !
Cats !
They purr
and press
and swish
against you
They tease
and taunt
and test
your disposition
and your patience
to get what it is
that cats want
Cats !
Felines !
Cats !
They purr
and press
and swish
and act like
Cats !

My Story

If I tell you a story
Will you follow the light
that it brings to my eyes
and will you connect with
the rhythm of the sounds
forming the picture of my words

If I tell you a story
Will you hear the pain
that is wrapped around my heart
and know such cords cannot
restrain the inevitable joy
encased in every story

If I tell you a story
Will you accept my tears
and laugh in my laugh
Will you fill with the treasure
of the gift I share

And if I tell you a story
If I tell you
my story
Will you tell me
yours

Let's Build A House

Let's build a house
Let's build
just a little house
Let's build a house
with many, many, rooms
and lots of space
to move in private thoughts
that still lead to a common threshold
Let's build a house
with tall, tall, windows
reflecting the seasons of nature's gifts
reminding how we link
to all that's life
Let's build a house
with wide swinging doors
welcoming sisters and brothers
and others we reach out to
(Let's bring in the whole world)
Let's build a house
that sings
and crys
and prays
and laughs
Let's build a house
that dances
as we struggle
as we hope

Let's build a house
Let's build
just a little house
Let's build a house
And let us call it home

Sisters and Brothers

Dancing In The Streets

I go to the streets
to dance with you
to create a parade
of music and laughter
and freedom

Another day I go
to the streets
to dance with you
But the air is heavy
with emptiness
The streets are cold with quiet
The parade fades

So each day I go
to the streets
not to dance
but to clean, to heal
and to wait
for the parade

One day I will go
to the streets
to dance with you
in music and laughter and freedom
that create the parade
when we dance

Who Tells A Rose

Who tells a Rose
when to bloom
The birth is imperceptible
We simply witness a burst
of color
The foliage performs
And routines adjust

Who tells a Rose
when to bloom
The schedule's not contested
We cast the usual glance
in awe
The foliage performs
and routines adjust

Who tells a Rose
when to bloom
The variety determines itself
Yet gives back ten-fold
of its fruit
The foliage performs
and routines adjust

Who tells a Rose
when to bloom
That work of art is patterned

The sacred mold is immune
to duplication
The foliage performs
And routines adjust

Who tells a Rose
when to bloom
We rush to nourish a gift
in hopes to preserve
a delicate treasure
The foliage performs
And routines adjust

Who tells a Rose
when to bloom
She's a God-sent phenomenon
Each petal's a snowflake
of love
The foliage performs
And routines adjust

Who tells a Rose
when to bloom . . .

I Like Us

I like us
I like our laughter
that rises between us
carrying us in its burst
allowing us to dwell
in every scatter of its
joy

I like us
I like our talk
Sharings between us
Stories in our lives
not yet complete
'til one conveys it to
the other

I like us
I like our touch
A closeness that merges
our souls
A blending of heartbeats
giving symmetry to
thoughts and words
giving comfort, rest
and peace

I like us
I like our calm
The quiet between us
that allows us to listen
That stillness between us
that helps us to hear

I like us
I like the two of us
I like us
I like the oneness of us

Women Standing

We are women
standing
facing days that
weigh upon us
enduring nights that
hold our abandon
Oh, we are women
fighting
refusing to accept
lives that bring
no gains
We give ourselves our hope
And we are women
dreaming
reaching hands
to men and children
clasping for that
circle of strength
But we are women
fearing
that our own power
will beat us down
that claiming our right to choose
will distance others from us
Yes, we are women
praying

Keeping vigils of our faith
learning we can sit and rest
and still know
we are women
standing

Sister Take My Coat

Sister, take my coat
You're cold in this wind
I'll stay inside by the fire
Don't notice that the coat is worn
with holes and rips
and shrunken from the wash
I'll be inside where it's warm

Sister, take my coat
You're wet in this rain
I'll take comfort in my quilt
Don't mind that the coat is thin
and can't repel the water
and wasn't made for one your size
I'll just cuddle in my soft chair

Sister, take my coat
You're naked in this heat
I'll relax on my porch
Don't bother that the coat
doesn't cloak your body and
can't protect from insect bites
I'll just sip a cool drink
under my fan

Sister take my coat
It's not brand new enough
for me
But it will suit you fine

Woman You Bother Me

Woman you bother me
with your silent moans
Staring out that window
Nose pressed to the glass
Not knowing what you're
looking for
Woman you bother me
with your hushed cries
Moving in this kitchen
like something else is directing
your hands to stir a pot
or push a broom
Moving from remote control
and can't find the button to stop
Woman you bother me
with your empty talk
Chilling sounds that rush
a squint to my eyes
Babbling words that
stumble on each other
gushing from you meaninglessly
Woman you bother me
with your living
cause I just can't stand
to see myself
in you.

Girl, Listen

Girl, listen to this,
They say we can't call ourselves "girls"
when us girls talking
They say we send the wrong message —
that we don't think too much of ourselves
that we maybe don't feel we more than girls
when we all womenfolk
They say maybe we don't know yet
that we big enough to be more than girls
that we good enough to be more than girls
Well, girl, let me tell you,
When us girls be talking
we in our own world
We talk by our own rules
and don't nobody else
suppose to be listening at us talk
no how
And girl, I been thinking about all
that they say
And we know that they ain't been there
to feel the warmth among us
when us girls be talking
And we know that they ain't been there
to sense the strength we share
in the stories between us
And we know that they surely ain't been there
to know how we can take the hurt and the joy

from deep down inside us
to build that special bond that ties us together
when us girls be talking
Girl, I say its our own way
I say its our own choice
And I say it ain't for them to say how we talk
But . . . at times I do think
it may be time for us to call ourselves
by the same name we'd choose to answer to
Sister, what you think

Searching for My Sister

I'm searching
for my sister
Have you seen her
I'm searching
for my sister
Have you heard her
I'm searching
for my sister
Have you felt her spirit

Her color
is in the sun
Her smile
accents the rainbow
Her dreams
are carried in the wind
I'm searching
for my sister
Do you know her

She pains
when a child cries
She trembles
when a brother is lost
She is raised in sorrowful moans
when she can't find
her sister

I'm searching
for my sister
Does she live in you

I'm searching
for my sister
Don't you see her
I'm searching
for my sister
Don't you hear her
I'm searching
for my sister
When you find her
Will you share her
with me

The Brother's Entitlement

I like to address the African American man
with his title
like Mister, and Sir
or Doctor, and Attorney
It pleasures me to say to
the African American man: Judge, Justice, Honorable
and especially, Your Honor
Oh, I like the sound of Councilman, Commissioner
Senator, Representative, Congressman
and President
coming before the African American man's name
When I say these words
it's like part of that African American man's name
has burst from a package that was bound
and buried for too long
It's not the title that
makes the man
Like it's not the name that
makes the person
It's the opportunity that ain't been his
It's the freedom he didn't know
came with his birth
I feel such pride
when I address my African American brother
with his title
Such joy is only matched
when I hear my brother
address my sister
with the same love

The Banquet Table

I like the way
he cares for her
His banquet table
is always spread
and he is there
to sit with her
to pass a dish
to fill a glass
to serve what
she may need
I like the way
he cares for her
but, then, I wonder
Is her table
set for him

Standing So Tall

You were so tall
standing
smiling shyly
in the shadow
yet not behind
the stature of another

You were so tall
standing
listening intently
taking in
with examining eyes
the wisdom of another

You were so tall
standing
following purposefully
using your own gifts
as you learned
in the experience of another

You were so tall
standing
guiding gently
giving in your commitment
to serve humbly
with your own special caring

You are still so tall
standing
now leading
more secure in you
and in all you have
to give

Talking Inside Myself

In One Breath

A cry
    A sigh
        A whimper
            A murmur
                A whisper
                    A whine
                        A moan
                            A groan
                            A death

A laugh
    A smile
        A grin
            A glow
                A cheer
                    A giggle
                      A jest
                        A breath
                          A life

Inside Myself

I been inside myself too long
feeling safe and feeling hid
I been inside myself too long
feeling nothing and missing all
Then you come along
and get inside myself
And there ain't room for two
inside myself
So we come out
And I know there ain't been room
for one inside myself
And so we try to make
a whole new self

Waiting

Seems like I am always waiting
Waiting for something that's promised
if I wait
Waiting for something that I know is
coming
if I wait
Waiting for something that I won't get
if I don't wait
So I am always waiting
Waiting to know
what I am waiting for

The Day To Make It Through

Do you ever get a day
when you just hurting all over
Ain't nothing wrong with you
You just aching
and you want to squeeze your arms
or wring your hands to feel a pain outside
to stop the pain inside
Do you ever get a day
when you locked up in yourself
and you can't break through
You moving
But you aint getting nowhere
You thinking but you just ain't
making no sense
Do you ever get a day
when you want to just step back
and start all over
Hoping you'll find where you
want to be
Knowing so little how
to get there
Do you ever get a day
when you feel like punching the air
Trying to burst the bubble
before it closes in on you
under the weight of your own helplessness
and despair

Do you ever get a day
when you know if you just make it
through
the rest is going to be all right
Cause you will always be struggling
But you won't always be hurting

Just One Day

Is one day too
much to ask
for
when a lifetime
is at stake
Is a lifetime
over time
to plan for
when one day
is at hand

I want one day
in a lifetime
to live
I want one day
to grow, to feel
to give

I want one day
in a lifetime
to cry
I want one day
to mourn, to grieve
to sigh

I want one day
in a lifetime
to smile
I want one day
to laugh, to rest
a while

I want one day
in a lifetime
Just one day
to be
me

I Come As The Rainbow

I come as the rainbow
in the same prescribed hues
signaling tranquility yet
never assuring the same

I come as the rainbow
melting in thinning trails
enticing smiles and embraces
causing sighs as well

I come as the rainbow
welcomed with sunrays
enjoyed for the moment yet
never longed for in absence

I come as the rainbow
a comfort to all in view
undetected in origin and
unheralded in leave

I come as the rainbow
multi-colored beauty of a rose
moist and refreshing
temperamental and ending

I come as the rainbow
reflective of true sensitivity
appearing as awesome delight
fading in the dust that I am

Who Died

Who died,
I ask
I feel the grief
all over me
I'm all into the mourning
The loss drains me
Who died,
I ask
It must have been
someone close to me
Who died,
I ask
There is an emptiness
returned in me
Nothing is the same
Who died,
I ask
Could it have been
me

The Mirror

Who wants to look
into a mirror anyway
What one wants to see
isn't there
And what one ought to see
is overlooked
So who would want to look
into a mirror anyway

There's this image of body
which does nothing separate
from one's own motions
So as one controls the mimicking
reflection
So does one determine what's good
and what's not so good
in the looking glass

Who wants to look
into a mirror anyway
What one sees when truly looking
can cause a sun-glaring
flinch
or even a thrust at one's
life
hoping to break
the pane

You need not look
into a mirror
Just look into the face
of another
When you see your love there
You will see yourself,
your image
Who needs to look
into a mirror anyway

When I'm Tired

When I'm tired, really tired
I sometimes sense a force of energy
separate from myself
bearing on myself
fueling a motion within myself

When I'm tired, really tired
I sometimes find myself
caught in this rush to give more
busying myself
engaging a body independent of a
mind

When I'm tired, really tired
I sometimes hear myself
listening for that outside call
hoping not to recognize its voice
knowing there'll be no will to refuse

When I'm tired, really tired
I sometimes realize I'm too tired
too tired to direct myself to rest
that I'm needing to be overcome
by just one more task

When I'm tired, really tired
I sometimes feel I'm someone else
separate from myself
fueling a motion within myself

When I'm tired, really tired
I never want to stay
so tired

Trainrides

Trainrides
show you the backside of life
Trainrides
show you the backyards of homes and schools
the backroads of factories, stores
and public buildings
Trainrides
show you the backdoors for employees
and delivery persons
the back porches of the elderly and pets
and garages filled with tools, toys
newspapers and boxes

Trainrides
show you the backside of life
fenced in
the playgrounds of homes, schools and parks
fenced in
the service entrances and loading docks
fenced in
the emergency entrances and exits
fenced in
Trainrides
show you the backside of life
that keeps you fenced out

Trainrides
show you everything that goes nowhere
Trainrides
show you junkyards and trash piles
the rundown buildings overcrowded or abandoned
Trainrides
show you the squatting smokers amidst
empty bottles and cans
Trainrides
show you your road to nowhere

Trainrides
show you the backside of life
Trainrides
show you paths to stumble into town
and paths to sneak out of town
Trainrides
show you all that's over your shoulder
that you walk away from
Trainrides
make your backside of life
your frontside

The Wise Person

If I were
a wise person
who had lived a long long time
and someone asked me
What is the secret
of your longevity
I would say
I try to remember
to take myself seriously
and to laugh at myself
whenever I do

God And Me

Waitin Fo God

You waitin fo God
Well, He ain't gon be there tonight
He gone
He gone on vacation or somethin
Oh, He be back
He always be back
No, can't say as I know
how long it'll be
It may be a long time, tho
I reckon He needs Hisself some res
We bothers Him so much

Last time I talked wit Him
He didn't sound so good
He sound kinda down, ya know,
Like He got somethin powerful strong
on His mind

You thinks maybe He sick
God do get sick, ya know
One time when I was talkin
with Him, I says:
Lord, how ya doin today
He says:
Ain't doin too well
I got dis killin headache and there's some
sharp pain in my stomach

I says:
Lord, I'm sho sorry to hear dat
What you doin fo yourself
Is there somethin I can do fo ya

Then He clears His throat and
His voice get a lil stronger
and He sort of roars out at me:
I is God, ya know!
Can't nobody do nothin fo God!
I gots to do it all fo myself!
But sometime I jes don have
no time to do nothin fo myself

I felt right sorry fo God
listening to Him go on like dat
I made myself a lil prayer right den,
Dat I was gon try to go easy
on the old Fellow, with my complaints
and all

I spect it gon be a lil quiet round here,
I mean with God gon and all
You see, the folks dey's kinda strange
at times
When dey knowed God at home and
Dey knowed He be lookin at 'em
and listenin at 'em dey goes
right on with dey devilment
And when dey feel dey maybe

done did a lil too much, ya know,
played too close in the devil's hand,
Dey goes crawlin to God, all sorrowful
and cryin on dey knees,
Lookin right pitiful
And God, He forgive 'em every time

But now, God, He ain't here,
And the folk is scaid
Dey ain't scaid to do no wrong, no,
Dey is scaid God jes might not
be back when dey needs to go
crawlin and cryin on dey knees
Like dey is sorry

God, He ain't here
And He don leave nobody
to fill in fo Him, neither
He tricky like dat sometime
I bet He sittin somewhere
sippin some cool wine,
countin His stars
And jes laughin at us down here,
Sayin to Hisself:
Dem damn fools, dey makes it so hard
on deyselves

Or maybe He lookin over us all
and jes shakin His head,
Dis-gusted at how we done
messed up His world

Well, Lord, If you have a mind to hear me,
I'm wishin ya have yoself
a mighty good time, wherever you be
But don be forgettin bout
us poor, sad folk down here
I knowed we think
we big stuff sometime
An we act like it's our world
an can't nobody else do nothin in it
lessen we tell 'em

But Lord ya know
livin ain't easy,
But hard as it be
ain't too many of us ready
to do no dying either

Yeah, we gon keep trying, Lord
We gon keep trying to do like ya say
an act like we got some good sense
Jes don be forgettin to come back, Lord
We be keepin your house warm
til you gets back

God, He ain't here
He gone
But He be back
He always be back

Lord, Are You There

Lord, are you there
I just need to know
you there
When the sea is calm
and the wind is mild
I know such peace
is yours
But when the water is rough
and the boat jostles me
I need to know you there

I ain't asking for no hand
on my shoulder
Or no blast of light
from the skies
(Don't scare me like that)
I just want that feeling inside
that say you ain't left me
and you going to help me

I guess you know me, Lord
So you know why I'm asking
You know it ain't cause
I think you ain't here
But you say you stay with those
who keep the faith
And I keep asking to let you know
I do believe in you

So, Lord, are you there
I just need to know
you there

Ain't God Somethin

Ain't God somethin
Ain't He tho
You forgets about
Him sometime
an befo you
knowed it
you needin Him
again
An you goes to
callin on Him
an he don't say
no
He can't say
no
Na, ain't He
somethin

An there's times
you hopin He
Ain't around
so you can
carry-on the way
you likes
An sho enough
He lets you know
He sees you
an then you

acts like you
don't know no
better for what
you doin
An he gives you
another chance
Just like befo
Na, ain't God
somethin

Then there's times
when everything's
goin right
An you wonders
why
But you don't wonder
long
cause right away
you knowed
He's come through
again
just like befo
Na, ain't He
somethin

It's a shame, tho
that we can't
love each other
when things is up
And love each other
when things is down

An it's a pity
that we can't give
a little
when we gets
so much
Na, ain't we
somethin
Ain't we tho

The Weariness On Me

Oh, Lord, the weariness done
come down on me again
I'm not seeing things so clearly
and I'm not knowing
what I'm feeling
I just want to stand still
holding my self quiet
so as I can find you
I try not to breathe
and stir up anything
I close my eyes to shut out
all outside me that ain't life
I try to focus my ears to
watch the clear sound coming through
My tongue don't speak but
my heart cry and cry

Oh, Lord, the weariness done
come down on me
I hold my self quiet
so as I can find you

My feet won't go nowhere
even when they moving
and my mind ain't accepting
nothing else that try to touch me
I hold my lips together like that's

all it takes to stop the time
I was left where there was no light
and I'm waiting for the day
to see me

Oh Lord, the weariness done
come down on me
I hold my self quiet
so as I can find you

The Lord Don't Like Ugly

The Lord don't like ugly
cause the Lord didn't make
nothing ugly
The Lord don't like oppression
cause the Lord didn't make
that either
We been beautiful and we been free
all the time
These came with our birth
Our mothers knew it
But our fathers couldn't talk about it
We been beautiful and we been free
all the time
We just got to believe it now
and act like we know it
The Lord didn't make nothing bad
and everything the Lord made
got something to do
We been good and we been gifted
all the time
These came with our birth
Our mothers knew it
But our fathers couldn't talk about it
We been good and we been gifted
all the time
We just got to choose now
how our lives will show it

The Creator

I know my Lord
is Creator
And I'm so glad my Lord
has such an imagination
Who else
would have thought of all those
shades of green and brown and
blue
Who else
would have thought of all those
diverse creatures of the universe

I know my Lord
is Creator
And I'm so glad my Lord
has such a sense of humor
Who else
would have thought
to put people in this world

I know my Lord
is Creator
And I'm so glad my Lord
cares about me
Who else
would have known that
I needed you

Let Your Child Cry

Lord, your child is crying
No tears flow
No sounds emerge
And the body is without motion
But in this temple
hide storms of tension
knotting nerves, constricting muscle,
unsteadying reason

Lord, your child is crying
And in this temple
hide clouds of fear
weighing down, obstructing vision,
obscuring reality

Lord, your child is crying
For in this temple
hide bolts of pain
striking flesh, disabling joints,
disillusioning right

Oh, Lord, your child is crying
Hiding in this temple
Thunder clashes
Lightning flashes
Rushing rain smashes
Lord, your child is crying

Lord, let these waters flow
that the rivers will calm
Let the clouds lift,
the thunder quiet,
and let the biting lightning fade
that the sun may shine
Lord, let your child cry

Just A Little Water

Lord, give me a little water
My throat is dry and parched
Lord, give me just a little water
Pour it on me, Lord
Til it drenches through my soul

Remember me God

I hope God remembers me
just in case no one else does
Even if someone remembers me
only God would truly know me
Only God has known my secrets
before I've completed them
in my mind
Only God can tell a truth in me
when I seem lost in deception
Only God knows what I intended
and only God knows why
Only God can help me find out
why I'm here
and only God can help me
meet that task
So I hope God remembers me
just in case no one else does
and I hope God remembers me
especially when I'm not appreciating
who I am

A Face for God

What face do you wear
when you're meeting with God
Is it calm, serene
affecting a preparedness
Is it blank, pale
rigid in uncertainties
Is it limp, haggard
lifeless in resignation
What face do you wear

What face do you choose
when you're meeting with God
Do you primp and paint
Do you shade and gloss
Do you scrape and pluck
Do you steam and stretch
What face do you choose

Do you wear a face
filled with all seasons
A face reflecting anything
you may need
A face ready to smile
to sorrow, to pray, to plead
What face would you show God
Can you find a face
that glitters, glows

and dances in joy
Can you find a face
that's hopeful, faith-filled
and giving in love
Can you find a face
that welcomes God

What face do you wear
when you're meeting with God
Is it an old face
you used to wear
Is it a new one
you haven't yet tried
Is it a face you own
or do you choose a mask
What face will God see

Listening For God

I listen so hard
sometimes
just to hear God
But I create such
a clamor
inside myself
that I often
miss the message

I listen so hard
sometimes
just to hear God
that I begin
to tell God when to speak
I say
God, talk to me
I need you to talk to me
I never consider
God might not have
anything to say
right then

I listen so hard
sometimes
just to hear God
that I even tell God
what to say

I say
God, tell me
I'm doing the right thing
Tell me
I'm doing what you want
Tell me
everything will be all right

I listen so hard
sometimes
just to hear God
But I create such
a clamor
inside myself
that I often
miss the message

So if you want to hear
What God has to say
you've got to stop
listening
to yourself

The Lord Do Just That

Sometimes the Lord
allows the earth to open wide
and swallow up everything
standing, sitting and lying about
while the dividing ground
kills, maims and in its tremor
claims for itself histories,
prosperities, futures, hopes and dreams
We don't know why
the Lord do that
The Lord just do that

Sometimes the Lord
permits the ocean
to slap itself across the land
washing up everything in its path
Dragging back into its bowels
the wretched and the innocent,
heroes and villains,
the unborn and the aged
We don't know why
the Lord do that
The Lord just do that

Sometimes the Lord
lets the blazing hot sun

dry up the riches of the soil
preventing grain and fruit to flourish
Causing the swells of hunger
as diseased bodies cry for death
while still clinging to life
scraping barren fields fit only for the wind
We don't know why
the Lord do that
The Lord just do that

Sometimes the Lord
stands back from the skies
and let loose torrents of rain
causing rivers to overflow
displacing roots and bonds of a people
Scaring us all to thinking
we may need to repeat Noah's task
and build ourselves a boat
We don't know why
the Lord do that
The Lord just do that

And we see that sometimes the Lord
allows every green thing
living by the hand of the Lord
to take fire and burn to a crisp
Laying to waste a land and a people
and disorienting those helpless creatures
that relied on bed and board
from a once lush forest

We don't know why
the Lord do that
The Lord just do that

Sometimes the Lord's eyes
must be closed
when brothers kill brothers
sisters spite sisters
husbands and wives dishonor a tie
and fathers, mothers, sons and daughters
swear enmity and these things
discredit a justice and deny a peace
We don't know why
the Lord do that
The Lord just do that

But as the Lord allows
all these things
The Lord also endows
The Lord puts in us
a will to live
a special power to forgive
and a gift to love
We don't know why
the Lord do that
The Lord just do that

Reaching
and Searching

I Knew You Once

I searched for you
but you weren't there
I planned for you
hoping you would come
I've lived years since then
expecting to find you

I feel people all around me
looking everyway
looking like you
I still dream of you
needing you with me
I still sigh for you
knowing you're out of my
reach
I've died years since then
having lived without you

I sense bodies drawing near me
strange with every touch
No touch is yours

I won't find you now
Your dust is the earth
Nor will I forget you ever

Your love is my breath
I live in my longings
accepting I knew you once

Aging Quietly

A few strains
of my hair
have turned gray
Sometimes
I see them
Sometimes
I don't

When You Get Lost

Tell me what you do
when you get lost
Tell me

Tell me what you feel
How things look to you
What happens in your head
What you say to yourself
Tell me

Can you see anything
when you get lost
Can you hear what's about you
Do you perceive life at all
Tell me

Tell me what scares you most
when you get lost
Can you draw from deep inside
What you use to hold you up
Do you move yourself differently
Tell me

Tell me what you do
to reach that special calm
Can you direct a prayer
When do you know to wait

When do you know to risk
Tell me

Tell me what you do
when you get lost
Tell me

Then tell me
How you know
When you not lost
no more
Tell me

To Prime A Heart

The strain I feel
on my heart
resounds like the gasping breath
of a well struggling to give
when there's no
water to prime
the pump

Life In A Mist

Sometimes I wish my life
were like a dream—
hazy, foggy, floating
And I wouldn't mind
the scary parts
because I'd know
eventually
I'd wake up

The Last Cry

I cried today
I felt the tears all over me
though my eyes were dry
and my face was unsmeared
I cried today
I could tell from
the heaviness in my heart
and the tremble in my throat
and the weakness in my knees
I could tell from
the downward rush
of my leading spirits
and the cloudy overcast
of my own smiles
and the dragging limpness
of my movements
I cried today
and I cried so hard
hoping to be all cried out
by tomorrow

I Know My Pain

My pain wraps around me
like barbed wire circling a pole
But the pole is motionless and unfeeling
I am flesh I tear

My pain swoops down on me
clutching with predator's claws
piercing and holding on
I feel like the helpless prey

My pain approaches as an element of my environment
only to devour in a gulp
My pain is not part of the ecological balance
But I feel like the smaller fish

My pain confines as a bird caged
as a dog leashed
as a horse bridled
as an ox yoked
I may appear free and in charge
but my pain disarms me

Even as I fear the thought of pain,
the memory of pain, the threat of pain
I am a formidable opponent of pain
I run and hide
I know my pain

Heaven's Drop

I'd like a drop
from heaven's cup
in my life right now
not to cleanse the world
but to wash me

World Of Heart

My heart holds up
everything in my world
But what holds up
my heart
in my world

Leaning on the Motherland

Children Of Africa

Come children I call you
Come to the land of your birth
Come to the soil of your mothers
Come to the skies of your fathers
Come children I call you
This earth holds your future
One field beckons to be sown
Another awaits chopping
Orchards need pruning and
vines need aligning
Come children
the yams are swelling the ground while
the corn is bursting from its cloak
Come children
When the rivers spill
the lowlands nurture rice paddies
Come children
The udders are heavy in milk
rivaled in sweetness only by the coconut fruit
Come children
All this is yours for a care
Come children I call you
Come to the faith that bore nations
Come to the pride that held a people in peace
Come to the God who awaits us
All this is yours for a love
Come children
We need you

My Africa

Africa
is my grandmother
that lonely rock
that only rock
that waves wash against
bruise against
and inevitably
calm against

Africa
is my mother
that conceiving earth
that revealing earth
that time directs from
measures out
and assuringly
moves ahead

Africa
is my self
that vagrant soul
that mocking soul
that winds heave homeward
breathe homeward
and untiringly
lifts to life
Africa

My Africa
that unchanging face
disfigured in a race
beguiled
in tainted blood
(A people's ruse)
and unwittingly
bars my strain

Listen To Africa

Listen
to the people
of Africa
Listen
to the keepers of the Nile
the protectors of the Niger
Listen
to those who read the sands
and follow the snowcaps
Listen
to the people
of the rainforest
They are one
in all the rising sounds
and one in the sprinkling colors
Listen
to those who depend on the grasslands
They respect the limits of life
They guard the rules of the food chain
Listen
to the people
of Africa
People of many languages
one spirituality
People of many cultures
one humanness

Listen
to the people
of Africa
Hear them tell of their living
their movements for scores of generations
carrying Africa to other lands
birthing new people, new cultures
One spirituality
One humanness
Listen
to the people
of Africa
and you will know
there are no people
who are not
of Africa

East

East
Rising sun
First people first souls
Africa

Africa Births The Child

Africa births the child
but the child sleeps in
Alabama
Africa once joined cultures
in a spiritual land
but people are separated
to die in Alabama
We look to Africa
for our strength
but we build our hope
in Alabama
Africa births the child
but the child sleeps
in Alabama

My Continental Love

Africa, my continental love
I courted you, pursued you
wooed you with delicate sweets,
fragrant flowers and gentle poetry
I ached for you in sleepless nights
pleading with the moon, as the medium
of lovers, to carry my heart's
tender ballads to your shores
But you elude me, you escape me
hiding in the unpredictable currents
that soldier your coasts
Your own wailing songs still
beckon to me, teasing and arousing
and enticing me ever
Africa, oh my Africa
We shall forever be
betrothed

War and Peace

Don't Shoot

Don't shoot your brother
He might really be
your brother
And don't shoot your sister
She could be
your sister too

Is it our perception
that war gives
direction
to still those who
would not stay

Is it our assessment
That bombs fall
in resentment
of those who
would only be free

When the child screams
through the blood
who is there
to reach the swollen cry

Don't shoot your brother
Don't shoot your sister
Don't shoot

Peace Keeps Coming

They say Peace is coming
so I got my doors open
and my windows, too,
are raised

I'm having a party
to welcome in this Peace
Bringing in my family
and all the folk about
We will sing and dance
and we will cry and shout

They say peace is coming
so I've cook a special meal
and prepared cool, refreshing drinks

I'm having a party
to welcome in this Peace
Bringing in my friends
and all the folk about
We will sing and dance
and we will cry and shout

They say Peace is coming
The birds and flowers herald it, too,
and the sun is brighter
for it

They say Peace is coming . . .
But somebody's war
won't let it through

No War Today

Let's say
go home
The war is cancelled today
Go home
But
home is where there is no peace
After all,
the war started
at home
So
let's say
go home
and stop the war
Go home
and fight for justice
Go home
and plan for peace
Then maybe one day
We'll at least be able to say
at home
there is no war

Peace For The World

I wish this world
were made for peace
Then every struggle
would carry hope
Every pain would move
toward ease
And I would never
forget to smile
I wish this world
were made for peace
Then every child
could feel safe
And all people could grow
in trust
And no one would ever
forget to celebrate
I wish peace
were made for this world

Never Understand War

Don't talk to me
about war
I can't understand
war right now
My mother has a tumor on her liver
her colon is inflamed
and there's a fever raging in her body
Don't talk to me
about war
I can't understand
war right now
My daughter graduates
from college in May
And she's planning a huge church wedding
in July
then she goes to medical school
in September
Don't talk to me
about war
I can't understand
war right now
My son is eighteen and has just started college
But he leaves the library
to demonstrate against this threat of war
And my younger daughter
studies physics and creates a poem sometimes
I won't let war

take this from her
So don't talk to me
about war
I can't understand
war right now
African Americans still aren't assured
the right to vote
There aren't enough souplines
for the growing number of homeless
people
and babies are dying
without a chance to live
Don't talk to me
about war
I can't understand
war right now
War only destroys
Taking lives, land, resources and cultures
War only stops
living, learning, growing, and celebrating
Don't talk to me
about war
I can't understand
war right now
Don't talk to me
about war
I'll never
understand war

Struggling For Justice

Clotilde

Who be Clotilde
Where she come from
What she do
What she want

Clotilde she dis woman who wear dat rag
round her head
And how Clotilde tie that rag around her head
tell the folk how she might be feelin dat day
And how the folk might be feelin bout Clotilde

When folks want to preach Clotilde
Dey say:
How Clotilde got dat rag tie round her head today
One say:
Donno, ain't seen her yet dis mornin
Another say:
Don care, I ain't for no mess outa Clotilde today
But another say:
Oh, I don seen her and she got dat rag
round her head with the knot tie high and tight
It got her forehead creased with waves
like it the ocean itself
Den the folk know Clotilde be troubled
Dey know she be troubled bout
Somethin big
And dey don wanta act like they know
what Clotilde trouble be

Now when Clotilde wear dat rag round her head
and tie dat knot low backa her neck
she gon be peaceful and be bout helpin the folk
And you gotta let Clotilde
help you when she wanta help you
She gets dis smile all over her face
and it don go away
Her eyes look right through yours
when she talkin to you and
she gets about in slow motion and
she don stop doin things
She look like she rollin
Clotilde seek folk out when she got dat rag
round her head with the knot tie low backa her neck
It's like she gotta touch everybody
makin sure they still livin
But Clotilde don be looking like she livin
in this world

Sometimes dat rag round her head with dat knot
tie low backa her neck
get aloose a little bit
If you close enough you hear her start to hummin
If you not so close
you feel her start to hummin
Pretty soon a long note draws outa dat hummin and
Clotilde hold dat note and she hold dat note
The folk listen and wonder when she gon breathe
When Clotilde do let go that note
dat rag round her head

with dat knot tie low backa her neck
get loosa
Like Clotilde done got free
Like she done throwed her toubles away
Seem like the folk feel safer
when dat rag aint tie so tight roung her head

There be times when Clotilde wear dat rag
round her head and tie dat knot to a side
mostly covering one ear
Dem gold rings in her ears turn on the light in her eyes
Stars cover up her face
Folk know Clotilde ready to laugh
One say:
Clotilde bout to get herself a dancin partner
Another say:
Wonder who Clotilde gon be dancin with tonight
Sometime Clotilde hear what dey say and she laugh
But Clotilde don never take dat rag from
round her head

She might let some curls fall out
or a long braid might show up one day
dat's when she wear dat rag round her head and
tie dat knot up front over her eyes
Dat rag be folded so neat and dat knot tie
up front over her eyes be lookin like a light-tower
Now, folk like when Clotilde wear dat rag with the
knot tie up front over her eyes
Dey don't know why

Dey jes don say nothin
Seem like dey don even see it
Sometime it aint Clotilde dat be strange
Sometime it be the folk

Now, folk don like when Clotilde wear dat rag
round her head and tie dat knot in two knots
Clotilde hardly come out when she wear dat rag
round her head and tie dat knot in two knots
Dats when the folk know she tired
Clotilde might come to her porch when somebody
passin
She might say:
One a these is yo knot tie so tight on my head
Can't you feel it
Dats yo knot what you gon do about it
She don wait fo no answer
She never get no answer
The folk know she tired
Dey know she tellin dem:
When you gon get tired too
When you gon do somethin bout these troubles

Sometimes Clotilde wear dat rag round her head and
there don be no knot tie in it at all
It be jes one smooth somethin comin outa her face
can't tell where one stop for the other
Folk act like dey don know Clotilde
when she got dat rag tie round her head and
there don be no knot tie in it at all
Dey say:

Who be Clotilde
Where she come from
What she do
What she want

Sometime Clotilde hear 'em and she cry
She be so sad in her pain
Her tears go every which-a-way on her face
Dey even come outa dat rag she wear round her head
with no knot tie in it at all
If the folk would listen at her crying
dey could hear her praying
dey could hear her callin:
Can't nobody find dat knot to loosen dis rag
round my head
Can't nobody
Can't nobody find dat knot to loosen
these troubles round my people
Can't nobody

Who be Clotilde
Where she come from
What she do
What she want

Look At This World

Look at this world
and see a people
crying
as they gaze on
padlocked silos
bulging from green seeds
that yield tall harvest
Look at these people
and see a nation
dying
in its own
tears
as its people wrench
in pain from absent wringing
of idle hands
Look at this nation
and mourn the babe
born
in the midst
of plenty with nothing
to eat

Look at this world
We see its people
naked, cold and trembling
with fear of those who hold the key
to the bulging, padlocked

silos
Take up a nation
and rise from the slush
that your children
may live to feel a warm sun
Take up a people
Fill your hands
with each other's
That you will share
in the earth's bounties
you bled for
Take up a people
Look at this world
and build a nation

Show Me Who You Are

You ain't showed me nothing yet
When you smiling
cause the sun is shining
When you happy cause your day went right
You ain't showed me nothing yet
When you say
you got it together
cause you know
ain't nothing happening
And you think you free
when all you doing
is backing off
You ain't showed me nothing yet
til you live like you believe
in somebody
other than yourself
And you struggling
to make something right
somewhere in this world
You ain't showed me nothing yet
til you show me
who you are
and what you do

People's Performance

There ought not be stars
or moonlit nights
All days ought be cloudy
dismal and forboding
Flowers should shed their bright hues
and birds be silenced likewise
Then nature would be in accord
with people's performace

The Secret

It's a secret I'm telling you
about my sandbox
My daddy built it for the three
smaller children
Four boards he nailed together and
placed under the big oak tree
in our yard
It seemed so huge when he poured
that first wheelbarrow of sand
I pretended I had an entire beach
under that oak tree as I tried to bury
my long skinny legs in the sand
I couldn't imagine anything
making me happier
I thought I should hold my breath
and squeeze my hands forever
The best times in the sandbox were when my friend
Anna Bell came to play
I was shy but had a great imagination
Bell was bold and laughed at openly at me
The worst time was when my daddy said
Bell couldn't come again to play

Why, my eyes asked
she's not our kind of people, he said
Bell came again and my sister came out and warned.
Daddy will be home soon

I told Bell my daddy said
she couldn't come again to play

Why, her eyes asked
My eyes were confused
I only saw the sand plastered
to her legs and arms as she rose
from the andbox
Her shorts dripped sand as she walked away
I heard some words—Bell,
I won't tell anyone you're not
our kind of people
Bell was brave
She kept our secret

The Village

The old men among us
they hold our stories
Their wrinkled hands weep
as they stretch their shadows
Their aged eyes teach
in whispers and moans
We hear the smiles from cracked lips
gathering and weaving a lineage
with every sigh of "Back there when . . ."
and "There was a time . . ."
The old men among us
they live forever

All the women parading in our lives
fussing and bustling and ever praying
they give us the lighthouse
guiding in storms and in calm
whether or not we ask
They know our dreams
before we find ourselves awake
They hear our music
before the scores are played
They live to keep life
All the women in our lives
they wait forever

The children who play at our feet
their birth carried every treasure
they could possibly lose in life
Their agile limbs are slowed
by our disabling fears
But their persistent minds
tell them our tongues will lighten
somehow in truth
Their gift to us is hopefulness
and the energy we find in laughter and in joy
The children who play at our feet
they put the running in us

The young women and men who would be tall
they slide in circles and falsehoods
grasping for the soul that must be there
But they can rise in the old men's stories
and they can swell in the children's laughter
as they grow in the women's watch
Yes, their hometies are their only ties
And they cry the tears
that are the manna of the people
The young women and men who would be tall
they would be leaders.

When Will the People Learn to Live

When will it be
that a people will know
how to eat
and not worry about food
When will it be
that the rain can fall
and the wind can blow
not reminding
we have no home
When will it be
that children will grow
in learning and creating
with mind and body intact
When will we hear a song
that brings tears and smiles
together
When, oh when, will our living
make dying worthwhile

Celebrations

Celebration

There is power in celebration
when you celebrate
what's been good to you
There is joy in celebration
when you give
what has grown within you
There is hope in celebration
when you share
what speaks to who you are
There is beauty in celebration
when you sing aloud
what has been the smallest
song in your heart
There is love in celebration
when you commit that
Celebration is love

Visions

Visions
are clear
even as they change
Visions
hold truth
even as we search
for understanding
Visions
grow in depth
even as we doubt our paths
Visions
persist in us
even as others
strike against our cause
Visions
are born
of our spiritual histories
even as we question our sufferings
Visions
are directed missions
we are gifted to fulfill
Visions
are as clear
even as we change

Risking Choice

I chose a road
one day
a road unclear, unmarked
and not altogether smooth

I chose a road
one day
stumbling on familiar ground
grasping at anything for support

I chose a road
one day
traveling where I had not been
and not sure where the road might lead

I chose a road
one day
where sunshine and storms interchanged
testing my faith and my will

I chose a road
one day
fearing it could be the wrong road
hoping it would be the right road

I chose a road
one day
trusting someone had been there
before
and preparing that others may
follow me

I chose a road
one day
And I may still choose a better one
tomorrow
because I risked a choice
this day

Treasures We Gather

We gather treasures
all our lives
even when we don't know it
The moment determines
the treasure
Some moments never leave us
Some treasures last forever
We gather treasures
all our lives
What a blessing when we know it

Going Home

I'm going home, I've decided
To catch a glimpse
of a small woodframe house
lined with roses, azaleas, camellias
and peppermint tea
I'm going home
to a backyard forever with the sounds
of baby chicks, ducks and
an occasional pig
A backyard housing rabbits
a vegetable garden
a chinaberry tree
and perpetually covered laundry lines
I'm going home, I've decided
To climb to the top of the spreading oak
and spy on the neighbors
or maybe just to sit under the fig trees
I'm going home
To be consumed by the nightly aroma
of freshly cooked breads from the
around-the-corner bakery
that also produced the cinnamon rolls for
after-Sunday-morning-Mass breakfast
I'm going home, I've decided
To the kite-flying winds of March
which threatened to topple us off
the tallest tombs in the graveyard across the street

To April even when it didn't bring Easter
To Summer flavors of newly cut grass in June
To the brown hightop shoes, coveralls and
a birthday in March, April, May, June
August, September, October and November
I'm going home
to holiday December
To my Mother's gumbo after midnight Mass
and wonder again why the day after Christmas
wasn't as much fun as Christmas Day
I'm going home
to Saturday night smells of Sunday's dinner
I'm going home
to when it's not yet payday time
and supper is cornbread and syrup
I'm going home, I've decided
To the constant sound of my Mother's voice
her quilting voice
her cooking and cleaning voice
her working-for-the-church voice
her voice to my father which invariably brought
the clicking sound
of a door closing behind him
I'm going home
to six siblings crowded in two beds
laughing, playing, fussing, crying,
growing and saying goodbye
I'm going home
to the piano in the dining room
proudly displaying generations of photographs

To the attic fan I feared would suck me up
To the graveyard across the street
that tolerated our nighttime games
I'm going home, I've decided
To smell the 4 p.m. coffee
awaiting my father's return from work
I'm going home
to follow behind him
not too closely as he checked
the vegetable garden, the roses, the azaleas,
the camellias and the peppermint tea
I'm going home, I've decided
I'm going home
but I've not decided
when

Give Yourself Christmas

Did you ever cry
on Christmas
Can you remember
what made you so sad
What hid your sunshine
that you would cry
on Christmas

Did you ever cry
on Christmas
What did you do
with those feelings
that emptiness
that hole in your soul
so heavy
that you would cry
on Christmas

Did you ever cry
on Christmas
and did you store
those emotions in gift boxes
wrapped in flaming ribbons
Or did you hide those hurts
amidst the bright bulbs and tinsels
of the trimmed tree

Did you ever cry
on Christmas
Can you remember
what made you so sad
What crushed your hope
denied your peace
robbed you of all smiles
that you could only cry on Christmas

Did you ever cry
just 'til Christmas
Can you remember
what gave you that hope
what raised your sunshine
and filled your soul
that you would not cry again
on Christmas

Then give yourself
Christmas
over and over
again
and hold to its faith

Naming Myself

When you call me
you should know
I can only answer
as who I know
I am

When you call me
you should think
of what you've learned
from me who
I am

When you call me
you should feel
my value as basic
to the people of whom
I am

So when you call me
you can be hopeful
that I will answer

The Whipping Block

I am off the whipping block
I don't need to remember
who or what put me there
or who or what held me there
I am off
The scourging and the lashings are stopped
I am taking my life
and repairing my esteem
My eyes no longer watch my feet
My mind and my faith direct me now
I am off the whipping block
I don't need to remember
what I was punished for
or for how long
I am off
I lift myself
I am off the whipping block
and that's what I need to remember

Acknowledgments

I have written poetry since I was a child, and that poetry was only for me. I grew up feeling that my poetry alone sustained me, befriended me, and kept me safe. But I have come to know that, actually, I was limited by this self-imposed confinement.

Only in recent years have I been able to appreciate the encouragement and support of my family and special friends. From them I learned to share my poetry. Through them I have acquired the courage to hear, to feel, to know, and to accept that my poetry holds something for others as well.

I am grateful to you who helped me to come out of myself where I was not hid and to create a whoole new self with all of you in my life.

Thank you to my children, Rachel, Alexandra, and Simon; to my husband, John; to my parents and siblings; to my special friends.

CAROL PREJEAN ZIPPERT

About the Author

Carol Prejean Zippert, born and raised in Lafayette, Louisiana, has lived in the Black Belt of west Alabama since 1971. She has used her Ph.D. in education to lift the community by serving as college teacher, as president of a community-based college, and as a county school board member. She works extensively with children, cooperatives, and culture organizations. With her spouse, John Zippert, she publishes a community newspaper, the *Greene County Democrat*. Her three children and growing number of grandchildren are a special joy in her life.